Hats, Scarves & Cov

Indulge your love of crochet with these great-looking accessories from Melissa Leapman. Each design uses different stitches or techniques that you'll enjoy creating.

LOOK FOR THE CAMERA in our instructions and watch our technique videos made just for you! **www.LeisureArts.com/75547**

LEISURE ARTS, INC.
Maumelle, Arkansas

Basket Weave Set

EASY +

Finished Sizes

Scarf: 6½" wide x 38¾" long (16.5 cm x 98.5 cm)

Hat: Fits head circumference 20" (51 cm)

SHOPPING LIST

Yarn (Medium Weight) MEDIUM 4

[6 ounces, 315 yards
(170.1 grams, 288 meters) per skein]:

- ☐ Scarf - 2 skeins
- ☐ Hat - 1 skein

Crochet Hook

- ☐ Size H (5 mm)
  or size needed for gauge

Additional Supplies

- ☐ Yarn needle (for Hat)

GAUGE INFORMATION

In pattern,
12 sts and 12 rows = 3¾" (9.5 cm)

Gauge Swatch:
5" wide x 2¼" high (12.75 cm x 5.75 cm)

Ch 18.
Work same as Scarf for 7 rows: 16 sts.
Finish off.

STITCH GUIDE

FRONT POST DOUBLE CROCHET *(abbreviated FPdc)*

YO, insert hook from **front** to **back** around post of st indicated *(Fig. 4, page 45)*, YO and pull up a loop (3 loops on hook), (YO and draw through 2 loops on hook) twice.

BACK POST DOUBLE CROCHET *(abbreviated BPdc)*

YO, insert hook from **back** to **front** around post of st indicated *(Fig. 4, page 45)*, YO and pull up a loop (3 loops on hook), (YO and draw through 2 loops on hook) twice.

SINGLE CROCHET 2 TOGETHER *(abbreviated sc2tog)*

Pull up a loop in each of next 2 sc, YO and draw through all 3 loops on hook **(counts as one sc)**.

HALF DOUBLE CROCHET 2 TOGETHER *(abbreviated hdc2tog)*

★ YO, insert hook in **next** st, YO and pull up a loop; repeat from ★ once **more**, YO and draw through all 5 loops on hook **(counts as one hdc)**.

INSTRUCTIONS
Scarf

Ch 126.

Row 1 (Right side)**:** Dc in back ridge of fourth ch from hook and each ch across *(Fig. 1, page 44)*: 124 dc.

Note: Loop a short piece of yarn around any stitch to mark Row 1 as **right** side.

Row 2: Ch 2 **(counts as first hdc, now and throughout)**, turn; work FPdc around each of next 2 sts, ★ work BPdc around each of next 2 sts, work FPdc around each of next 2 sts; repeat from ★ across to last st, hdc in last st: 62 FPdc, 60 BPdc, and 2 hdc.

Repeat Row 2 until Scarf measures approximately 3¼" (8.5 cm) from beginning ch, ending by working a **wrong** side row.

Next Row (Keyhole Opening)**:** Ch 2, turn; ★ work FPdc around each of next 2 sts, work BPdc around each of next 2 sts; repeat from ★ 6 times **more**, ch 4, skip next 4 sts, work FPdc around each of next 2 sts, † work BPdc around each of next 2 sts, work FPdc around each of next 2 sts †; repeat from † to † across to last hdc, hdc in last hdc: 60 FPdc, 58 BPdc, 2 hdc, and 4 chs.

Next Row: Ch 2, turn; work FPdc around each of next 2 sts, ★ work BPdc around each of next 2 sts, work FPdc around each of next 2 sts; repeat from ★ across to next ch-4 sp, hdc in next 4 chs, † work BPdc around each of next 2 sts, work FPdc around each of next 2 sts †; repeat from † to † across to last hdc, hdc in last hdc.

Repeat Row 2 until piece measures approximately 6½" (16.5 cm) from beginning ch, ending by working a **right** side row.

Finish off.

Hat

Ch 65 loosely; being careful not to twist ch, join with slip st to back ridge of first ch to form a ring *(Fig 1, page 44)*.

Rnd 1 (Right side)**:** Ch 3 **(counts as first dc)**, dc in back ridge of next ch and each ch around; join with slip st to first dc: 65 dc.

Note: Loop a short piece of yarn around any stitch to mark Rnd 1 as **right** side.

Rnd 2: Ch 2 **(counts as first hdc, now and throughout)**, ★ work FPdc around each of next 2 sts, work BPdc around each of next 2 sts; repeat from ★ around; join with slip st to first hdc: 32 FPdc, 32 BPdc, and one hdc.

Rnd 3: Ch 2, ★ work BPdc around each of next 2 sts, work FPdc around each of next 2 sts; repeat from ★ around; join with slip st to first hdc.

Repeat Rnds 2 and 3 for pattern until piece measures approximately 5½" (14 cm) from beginning ch.

CROWN

Rnd 1: Ch 2, hdc2tog, (hdc in next 6 sts, hdc2tog) around to last 6 sts, hdc in last 4 sts, hdc2tog; join with slip st to first hdc: 56 hdc.

Rnd 2: Ch 2, hdc in next 4 hdc, hdc2tog, (hdc in next 5 hdc, hdc2tog) around; join with slip st to first hdc: 48 hdc.

Rnd 3: Ch 2, hdc in next hdc, hdc2tog, (hdc in next 2 hdc, hdc2tog) around; join with slip st to first hdc: 36 hdc.

Rnd 4: Ch 2, hdc2tog, (hdc in next hdc, hdc2tog) around; join with slip st to first hdc: 24 hdc.

Rnds 5 and 6: Ch 1, hdc in next hdc, hdc2tog around; skip beginning ch-1 and join with slip st to first hdc: 6 hdc.

Finish off, leaving a long end for sewing.

Thread yarn needle with long end and weave needle through sts on Rnd 6 *(Fig. 6, page 45)*; pull tightly to close and secure end.

TOPPER

Ch 2.

Rnd 1 (Right side)**:** 6 Sc in second ch from hook; join with slip st to first sc.

Note: Mark Rnd 1 as **right** side.

Rnd 2: Ch 1, 2 sc in same st as joining and in each sc around; join with slip st to first sc: 12 sc.

Rnd 3: Ch 1, sc in same st as joining, 2 sc in next sc, (sc in next sc, 2 sc in next sc) around; join with slip st to first sc: 18 sc.

Rnd 4: Ch 1, sc in same st as joining and in next sc, 2 sc in next sc, (sc in next 2 sc, 2 sc in next sc) around; join with slip st to first sc: 24 sc.

Rnds 5-7: Ch 1, sc in same st as joining and in each sc around; join with slip st to first sc.

Rnd 8: Ch 1, beginning in same st as joining, (sc2tog, sc in next 2 sc) around; join with slip st to first sc: 18 sc.

Rnd 9: Ch 1, beginning in same st as joining, (sc2tog, sc in next sc) around; join with slip st to first sc: 12 sc.

Stuff Topper with yarn.

Rnd 10: Ch 1, beginning in same st as joining, sc2tog around; join with slip st to first sc: 6 sc.

Finish off, leaving a long end for sewing.

Thread yarn needle with long end and weave needle through sts on Rnd 10; pull tightly to close and secure end, do **not** cut yarn. With same yarn end, sew Topper to top of Hat.

Embossed Ribs Set

EASY +

Finished Sizes

Scarf: 6½" wide x 72" long (16.5 cm x 183 cm)

Hat: Fits head circumference 20" (51 cm)

SHOPPING LIST

Yarn (Medium Weight) MEDIUM 4

[5 ounces, 251 yards
(142 grams, 230 meters) per skein]:

- ☐ Scarf - 3 skeins
- ☐ Hat - 1 skein

Crochet Hook

- ☐ Size J (6 mm)
  or size needed for gauge

Additional Supplies

- ☐ Yarn needle (for Hat)

GAUGE INFORMATION

In pattern,

12 sts (3 repeats) = 3¾" (9.5 cm);

8 rows = 3" (7.5 cm)

Gauge Swatch:

6½" wide x 3" high

(16.5 cm x 7.5 cm)

Work same as Scarf for 8 rows:
16 hdc and 5 FP Clusters.

STITCH GUIDE

FRONT POST CLUSTER

(abbreviated FP Cluster)

(uses one st)

★ YO twice, insert hook from **front** to **back** around post of st indicated one row **below** *(Fig. A)*, YO and pull up a loop even with loop on hook, (YO and draw through 2 loops on hook) twice; repeat from ★ once **more**, YO and draw through all 3 loops on hook. Skip st **behind** FP Cluster.

Fig. A

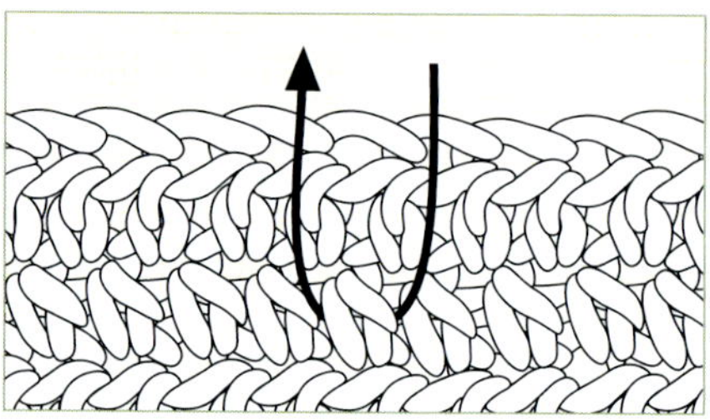

SINGLE CROCHET 2 TOGETHER

(abbreviated sc2tog)

Pull up a loop in each of next 2 sts, YO and draw through all 3 loops on hook **(counts as one sc)**.

INSTRUCTIONS

Scarf

Ch 22.

Row 1 (Right side)**:** Hdc in back ridge of third ch from hook **(2 skipped chs count as first hdc)** and in each ch across *(Fig. 1, page 44)*: 21 hdc.

Note: Loop a short piece of yarn around any stitch to mark Row 1 as **right** side.

Row 2: Ch 2 **(counts as first hdc, now and throughout)**, turn; hdc in next hdc and in each hdc across.

Rows 3 and 4: Ch 2, turn; hdc in next hdc, work FP Cluster around hdc one row **below** next st, ★ hdc in next 3 hdc, work FP Cluster around hdc one row **below** next st; repeat from ★ across to last 2 hdc, hdc in last 2 hdc: 16 hdc and 5 FP Clusters.

Row 5: Ch 2, turn; hdc in next hdc, work FP Cluster around FP Cluster one row **below** next st, ★ hdc in next 3 hdc, work FP Cluster around FP Cluster one row **below** next st; repeat from ★ across to last 2 hdc, hdc in last 2 hdc.

Repeat Row 5 until Scarf measures approximately 72" (183 cm) from beginning ch, ending by working a **right** side row.

Finish off.

Hat

BAND

Ch 14.

Row 1 (Right side)**:** Hdc in back ridge of third ch from hook **(2 skipped chs count as first hdc)** and each ch across *(Fig. 1, page 44)*: 13 hdc.

Note: Loop a short piece of yarn around any stitch to mark Row 1 as **right** side.

Row 2: Ch 2 **(counts as first hdc, now and throughout)**, hdc in next hdc and in each hdc across.

Row 3: Ch 2, turn; hdc in next hdc, work FP Cluster around hdc one row **below** next hdc, ★ hdc in next 3 hdc, work FP Cluster around hdc one row **below** next hdc; repeat from ★ once **more**, hdc in last 2 hdc: 10 hdc and 3 FP Clusters.

Row 4: Ch 2, turn; hdc in next hdc and in each st across: 13 hdc.

Row 5: Ch 2, turn; hdc in next hdc, work FP Cluster around FP Cluster one row **below** next hdc, ★ hdc in next 3 hdc, work FP Cluster around FP Cluster one row **below** next hdc; repeat from ★ once **more**, hdc in last 2 hdc: 10 hdc and 3 FP Clusters.

Repeat Rows 4 and 5 until Band measures approximately 20" (51 cm) from beginning ch when slightly stretched, ending by working Row 4: 13 hdc.

Joining Row: With **right** side of short edges together and working through **both** loops of each st on **both** layers, ch 1, slip st in each st across; do **not** finish off.

Turn Band **right** side out.

BODY

Rnd 1 (Right side)**:** Ch 2; with **right** side facing and working in ends of rows, work 55 hdc evenly spaced around; join with slip st to first hdc: 56 hdc.

Rnd 2: Ch 2, turn; hdc in next hdc and in each hdc around; join with slip st to first hdc.

Rnd 3: Ch 2, turn; hdc in next 2 hdc, work FP Cluster around hdc one rnd **below** next hdc, ★ hdc in next 3 hdc, work FP Cluster around hdc one rnd **below** next hdc; repeat from ★ around; join with slip st to first hdc: 42 hdc and 14 FP Clusters.

Rnd 4: Ch 2, turn; hdc in next st and in each st around; join with slip st to first hdc: 56 hdc.

Rnd 5: Ch 2, turn; hdc in next 2 hdc, work FP Cluster around FP Cluster one rnd **below** next hdc, ★ hdc in next 3 sts, work FP Cluster around FP Cluster one rnd **below** next hdc; repeat from ★ around; join with slip st to first hdc: 42 hdc and 14 FP Clusters.

Repeat Rnds 4 and 5 until piece measures approximately 7½" (19 cm) from bottom edge, ending by working Rnd 5; do **not** finish off: 42 hdc and 14 FP Clusters.

CROWN

Rnd 1: Ch 1, do **not** turn; beginning in same st as joining, (sc2tog, sc in next 5 sts) around; join with slip st to first sc: 48 sc.

Rnd 2: Ch 1, beginning in same st as joining, (sc2tog, sc in next 4 sc) around; join with slip st to first sc: 40 sc.

Rnd 3: Ch 1, beginning in same st as joining, (sc2tog, sc in next 8 sc) around; join with slip st to first sc: 36 sc.

Rnd 4: Ch 1, beginning in same st as joining, (sc2tog, sc in next 7 sc) around; join with slip st to first sc: 32 sc.

Rnd 5: Ch 1, beginning in same st as joining, (sc2tog, sc in next 6 sc) around; join with slip st to first sc: 28 sc.

Rnd 6: Ch 1, beginning in same st as joining, (sc2tog, sc in next 5 sc) around; join with slip st to first sc: 24 sc.

Rnd 7: Ch 1, beginning in same st as joining, (sc2tog, sc in next sc) around; join with slip st to first sc: 16 sc.

Rnd 8: Ch 1, beginning in same st as joining, sc2tog around; join with slip st to first sc: 8 sc.

Finish off, leaving a long end for sewing.

Thread yarn needle with long end and weave needle through sts on Rnd 8 *(Fig. 6, page 45)*; pull tightly to close and secure end.

BOTTOM TRIM

Rnd 1: With **right** side of Band facing and working in ends of rows, join yarn with sc at back seam *(see Joining With Sc, page 44)*; work 55 sc evenly spaced around; join with slip st to first sc: 56 sc.

Rnd 2: Ch 1; working from **left** to **right**, work reverse sc in each sc around *(Figs. 7a-d, page 46)*; join with slip st to first st, finish off.

Fair Isle Set

INTERMEDIATE

Finished Sizes

Scarf: 7½" wide x 62½" long (19 cm x 159 cm)

Hat: Fits head circumference 20" (51 cm)

SHOPPING LIST

Yarn (Medium Weight) MEDIUM 4

[3.5 ounces, 210 yards (100 grams, 192 meters) per skein]:

Scarf

- ☐ Color A (Grey) - 3 skeins
- ☐ Color B (Black) - 2 skeins
- ☐ Color C (Aran) - 1 skein
- ☐ Color D (Lt Red) - 1 skein
- ☐ Color E (Red) - 1 skein
- ☐ Color F (Dk Red) - 1 skein

Hat

- ☐ Color A (Grey) - 1 skein
- ☐ Color B (Black) - 1 skein
- ☐ Color C (Aran) - 1 skein
- ☐ Color D (Lt Red) - 1 skein
- ☐ Color E (Red) - 1 skein
- ☐ Color F (Dk Red) - 1 skein

Crochet Hook

- ☐ Size I (5.5 mm)
  or size needed for gauge

Additional Supplies

- ☐ Yarn needle (for Hat)

GAUGE INFORMATION

In Fair Isle pattern,
16 sc and 14 rnds = 4" (10 cm)
Gauge Swatch: 3" wide (flattened) x 2" high (7.5 cm x 5 cm)
With Black, ch 24.
Work same as Scarf, page 18, for 7 rnds: 24 sc.
Finish off.

— STITCH GUIDE —

SINGLE CROCHET 2 TOGETHER *(abbreviated sc2tog)*

Pull up a loop in each of next 2 sc, YO and draw through all 3 loops on hook **(counts as one sc)**.

FAIR ISLE

Fair Isle is a technique used to create patterns with many colors. Only two colors are used on each round and the unused color is worked over, weaving it into the fabric.

GAUGE WHILE CHANGING COLORS

For the stitches to look uniform and also for the project to match the finished size given in the instructions, it is essential to maintain stitch gauge while changing colors. You will also be assured that you have enough yarn to finish your project.

CHANGING COLORS

To change colors in sc, insert the hook in the next sc, YO and pull up a loop (2 loops on hook); drop yarn to **wrong** side of work, with new color, YO and draw through both loops on hook *(Fig. A)*.

Fig. A

To join a new color with a slip st, insert the hook in the first st of the rnd. Pick up the color specified, YO with the new color and draw it through the st and the loop on the hook *(Fig. B)*.

Fig. B

This method gives the joining a smooth look *(Fig. C)*.

Fig. C

When it's time to change to a previously used color, hold the yarn **loosely** on the **wrong** side of the work while drawing it up to join with slip st *(Fig. D)*.

Fig. D

Always keep the first color used in a round above the second color as you change colors no matter which color you are changing to *(Fig. E)*.

Fig. E

Yarn Floats are created when a color is carried **loosely** on the **wrong** side of the work *(Fig. F)*.

Fig. F

Work over the floats on the next round *(Fig. G)*, enclosing them within the fabric to prevent the yarn from showing on the front or back.

Fig. G

HOW TO FOLLOW A CHART

The chart shows each stitch as a square, indicating what color each stitch should be.

To keep your place, a ruler, piece of paper, or a sticky note can be placed **above** the round you are working. You need to see the round you have just completed to ensure you are working the correct color.

When working in rounds always follow each row of the chart from **right** to **left**.

INSTRUCTIONS

Scarf

With Color B, ch 60; being careful not to twist ch, join with slip st to back ridge of first ch to form a ring *(Fig. 1, page 44)*.

Rnd 1 (Right side)**:** Ch 1, sc in back ridge of same st as joining and each ch around; join with slip st to first sc: 60 sc.

The **right** side will always be facing you. When changing colors, drop yarn to **back** of work; do **not** cut yarn.

Rnd 2: Ch 1, sc in Back Loop Only of same st as joining and each sc around *(Fig. 2, page 44)*; join with slip st to first sc.

Only two colors are used per round. Change colors *(Figs. A-E, pages 16 and 17)* carrying the unused color **loosely** on the inside of the Scarf and working over the floats on subsequent rounds *(Figs. F & G, page 18)*. Yarn can be carried up 2 rounds. Cut yarns when they are no longer needed.

Rnd 3: Ch 1, working in Back Loops Only, sc in same st as joining and in next sc, sc in next sc changing to Color C, ★ sc in next sc changing to Color B, sc in next 2 sc, sc in next sc changing to Color C; repeat from ★ around to last sc, sc in last sc; join with slip st to first sc.

Rnds 4-18: Ch 1, sc in Back Loop Only of same st as joining and each sc around following Chart Rnds 4-18 *(see How to Follow a Chart, page 18)*; join with slip st to first sc.

COLOR KEY

- Color A ____________
- Color B ____________
- Color C ____________
- Color D ____________
- Color E ____________
- Color F ____________

Write the color name of the yarn you're using in the Color Key.

SCARF CHART

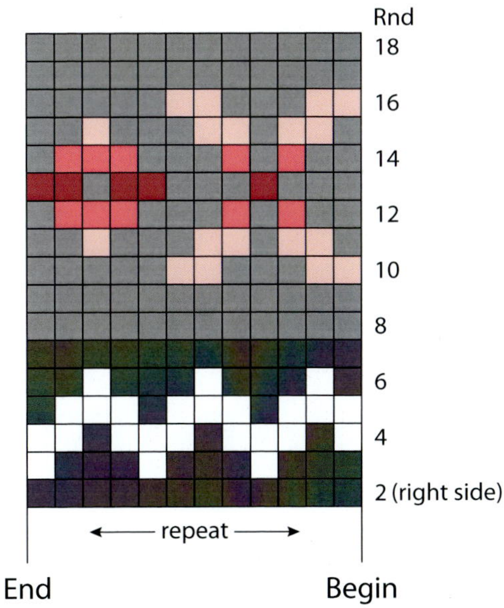

On all rounds, follow the Chart from **right** to **left**.

Repeat Rnds 2-18 until Scarf measures approximately 62" (157.5 cm) from beginning ch, ending by working Rnd 7.

Finish off.

Trim: Flatten Scarf with joining at center back. With front facing and working through **both** loops of each sc on **both** layers, join Color B with sc in first st at fold on last row ***(see Joining With Sc, page 44)***; sc in next st and in each st across; finish off.

Repeat for bottom edge.

TASSEL (Make 4)

Cut a piece of cardboard 3" wide x 5" long (7.5 cm x 12.5 cm). Wind a double strand of each color of yarn around the cardboard twice. Cut an 18" (45.5 cm) length of Color B and insert it under all of the strands at the top of the cardboard; pull up **tightly** and tie securely. Leave the yarn ends long enough to attach the tassel. Cut the yarn at the opposite end of the cardboard ***(Fig. H)*** and then remove it. Cut a 6" (15 cm) length of Color A and wrap it **tightly** around the tassel twice, 1" (2.5 cm) below the top ***(Fig. I)***; tie securely. Trim ends.

Attach one Tassel to each corner of Scarf.

Fig. H

Fig. I

Hat

RIBBING

With Color A, ch 8.

Row 1 (Right side)**:** Sc in back ridge of second ch from hook and each ch across *(Fig. 1, page 44)*: 7 sc.

Note: Loop a short piece of yarn around any stitch to mark Row 1 as **right** side.

Row 2: Ch 1, turn; sc in Back Loop Only of each sc across *(Fig. 2, page 44)*.

Repeat Row 2 until Ribbing measures approximately 20" (51 cm) from beginning ch when slightly stretched, ending by working a **right** side row.

Joining Row: Ch 1, turn; hold beginning ch and last row with **right** side together and working through **inside** loops of each st on **both** layers, slip st in each st across; finish off.

Turn Ribbing **right** side out.

BODY

The **right** side will always be facing you. When changing colors, drop yarn to **back** of work; do **not** cut yarn.

Rnd 1 (Right side)**:** With **right** side facing, join Color B with sc in seam *(see Joining With Sc, page 44)*; work 83 sc evenly spaced along end of rows; join with slip st to first sc: 84 sc.

Rnd 2: Ch 1, sc in Back Loop Only of same st as joining and each sc around; join with slip st to first sc.

Only two colors are used per round. Change colors *(Figs. A-E, pages 16 and 17)* carrying the unused color **loosely** on the **back** of the Hat and working over the floats on subsequent rounds *(Figs. F & G, page 18)*. Yarn can be carried up 2 rounds. Cut yarns when they are no longer needed.

Rnd 3: Ch 1, working in Back Loops Only, sc in same st as joining and in next sc, sc in next sc changing to Color C, ★ sc in next sc changing to Color B, sc in next 2 sc, sc in next sc changing to Color C; repeat from ★ around to last sc, sc in last sc; join with slip st to first sc.

Rnds 4-24: Ch 1, sc in Back Loop Only of same st as joining and each sc around following Chart Rnds 4-24 *(see How to Follow a Chart, page 18)*; join with slip st to first sc.

Finish off.

HAT CHART

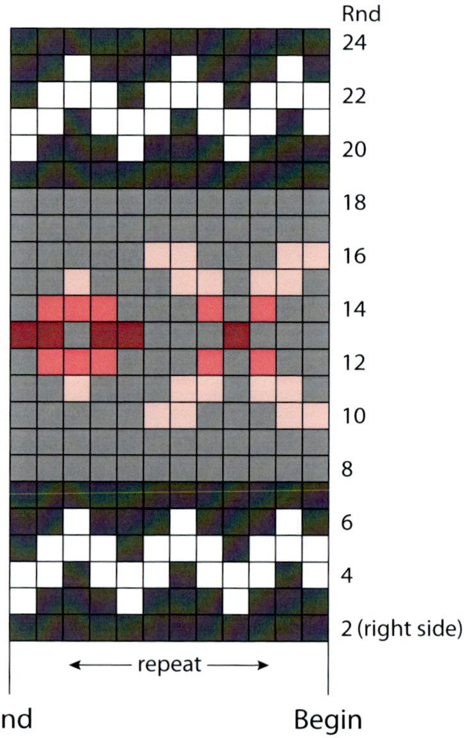

COLOR KEY

- Color A ______________
- Color B ______________
- Color C ______________
- Color D ______________
- Color E ______________
- Color F ______________

Write the color name of the yarn you're using in the Color Key.

On all rounds, follow the Chart from **right** to **left**.

CROWN

Continue to work in Back Loops Only throughout.

Rnd 1: With **right** side facing, join Color A with sc in same st as joining; sc in next sc and in each sc around; join with slip st to first sc.

Rnd 2: Ch 1, beginning in same st as joining, (sc2tog, sc in next 5 sc) around; join with slip st to first sc: 72 sc.

Rnd 3: Ch 1, beginning in same st as joining, (sc2tog, sc in next 4 sc) around; join with slip st to first sc: 60 sc.

Rnd 4: Ch 1, beginning in same st as joining, (sc2tog, sc in next 3 sc) around; join with slip st to first sc: 48 sc.

Rnd 5: Ch 1, beginning in same st as joining, (sc2tog, sc in next 2 sc) around; join with slip st to first sc: 36 sc.

Rnds 6 and 7: Ch 1, beginning in same st as joining, (sc2tog, sc in next sc) around; join with slip st to first sc: 16 sc.

Rnd 8: Ch 1, beginning in same st as joining, sc2tog around; join with slip st to first sc, finish off leaving a long end for sewing: 8 sc.

Thread yarn needle with long end and weave needle through sts on Rnd 8 ***(Fig. 6, page 45)***; pull tightly to close and secure end.

Little Glitzy Neckwarmer

EASY

Finished Size: 6½" wide x 32" long (16.5 cm x 81.5 cm)

SHOPPING LIST

Yarn (Medium Weight) MEDIUM 4

[3.5 ounces, 202 yards (100 grams, 185 meters) per skein]:

- ☐ 1 skein

Crochet Hook

- ☐ Size H (5 mm) **or** size needed for gauge

Additional Supplies

- ☐ 7/8" (22 mm) Buttons - 3.
- ☐ Sewing needle and matching thread

GAUGE INFORMATION

In pattern,
(dc, ch 1, dc) 3 times = 2" (5 cm);
6 rows = 2¾" (7 cm)

Gauge Swatch:
5¾" wide x 2¾" high
(14.5 cm x 7 cm)

Work same as Neckwarmer for 6 rows: 18 dc and 8 ch-1 sps.

STITCH GUIDE

PICOT

Ch 3, slip st in third ch from hook.

INSTRUCTIONS

Body

Ch 28.

Row 1 (Right side)**:** (Dc, ch 1, dc) in fifth ch from hook **(4 skipped chs count as first dc plus one skipped ch)**, ★ skip next 2 chs, (dc, ch 1, dc) in next ch; repeat from ★ across to last 2 chs, skip next ch, dc in last ch: 18 dc and 8 ch-1 sps.

Note: Loop a short piece of yarn around any stitch to mark Row 1 as **right** side.

Row 2: Ch 3 **(counts as first dc)**, turn; (dc, ch 1, dc) in each ch-1 sp across to last 2 dc, skip next dc, dc in last dc.

Repeat Row 2 until piece measures approximately 30" (76 cm) from beginning ch, ending by working a **wrong** side row; do **not** finish off.

Edging

Rnd 1: Ch 4 **(counts as first dc plus ch 1)**, turn; (dc, ch 1) twice in first dc, (dc in next ch-1 sp, ch 1) across to last 2 dc, skip next dc, (dc, ch 1) 3 times in last dc; working in ends of rows, dc in first row, ch 1, (dc in next row, ch 1) across; working in free loops of beginning ch *(Fig. 3, page 44)*; (dc, ch 1) 3 times in first ch, skip next ch, dc in next ch, ch 1, (skip next 2 chs, dc in next ch, ch 1) 7 times, skip next ch, (dc, ch 1) 3 times in next ch; working in ends of rows, dc in first row, ch 1, (dc in next row, ch 1) across; join with slip st to first dc.

Rnd 2: (Slip st, ch 1, sc, work Picot, sc) in next ch-1 sp, (sc, work Picot, sc) in next ch-1 sp and in each ch-1 sp around; join with slip st to first sc, finish off.

Using photo as a guide for placement, sew buttons evenly spaced across bottom edge.

To wear your Cowl as shown above, use ch-1 sps on Rnd 1 of Edging as buttonholes.

To wear your Cowl as shown on page 25, use ch-1 sps on Rnd 1 of Edging formed at the side edge as buttonholes.

Shaped Hat

EASY

Fits Head Circumference:
20" (51 cm)

SHOPPING LIST

Yarn (Bulky Weight) BULKY 5
[3 ounces, 144 yards
(85 grams, 132 meters) per skein**]**:
☐ 1 skein

Crochet Hook
☐ Size K (6.5 mm)
or size needed for gauge

GAUGE INFORMATION

12 sc and 13 rnds = 4" (10 cm)

Gauge Swatch:

2½" (6.25 cm) diameter

Work same as Hat Rnds 1-4: 32 sc.

INSTRUCTIONS

Rnd 1 (Right side)**:** Ch 2, 8 sc in second ch from hook; join with slip st to first sc.

Rnd 2: Ch 1, 2 sc in same st as joining and in each sc around; join with slip st to first sc: 16 sc.

Rnd 3: Ch 1, 2 sc in same st as joining, sc in next sc, (2 sc in next sc, sc in next sc) around; join with slip st to first sc: 24 sc.

Rnd 4: Ch 1, 2 sc in same st as joining, sc in next 2 sc, (2 sc in next sc, sc in next 2 sc) around; join with slip st to first sc: 32 sc.

Rnd 5: Ch 1, 2 sc in same st as joining, sc in next 3 sc, (2 sc in next sc, sc in next 3 sc) around; join with slip st to first sc: 40 sc.

Rnd 6: Ch 1, 2 sc in same st as joining, sc in next 4 sc, (2 sc in next sc, sc in next 4 sc) around; join with slip st to first sc: 48 sc.

Rnd 7: Ch 1, 2 sc in same st as joining, sc in next 5 sc, (2 sc in next sc, sc in next 5 sc) around; join with slip st to first sc: 56 sc.

Rnd 8: Ch 1, 2 sc in same st as joining, sc in next 13 sc, (2 sc in next sc, sc in next 13 sc) around; join with slip st to first sc: 60 sc.

Rnds 9-24: Ch 1, sc in same st as joining and in each sc around; join with slip st to first sc.

Rnd 25: Ch 1, 2 sc in same st as joining, sc in next 11 sc, (2 sc in next sc, sc in next 11 sc) around; join with slip st to first sc: 65 sc.

Rnd 26: Ch 1, 2 sc in same st as joining, sc in next 4 sc, (2 sc in next sc, sc in next 4 sc) around; join with slip st to first sc: 78 sc.

Rnd 27: Ch 1, 2 sc in same st as joining, sc in next 5 sc, (2 sc in next sc, sc in next 5 sc) around; join with slip st to first sc: 91 sc.

Rnd 28: Ch 1; working from **left** to **right**, work reverse sc in each sc around *(Figs. 7a-d, page 46)*; join with slip st to first st, finish off.

Tweed Set

EASY +

Finished Sizes

Cowl: 6½" wide x 56½" circumference (16.5 cm x 143.5 cm)

Hat: Fits head circumference 20" (51 cm)

SHOPPING LIST

Yarn (Medium Weight) 4

[3.5 ounces, 170 yards
(100 grams, 156 meters) per skein]:

Cowl

- ☐ Red - 1 skein
- ☐ Orange - 1 skein
- ☐ Green - 1 skein

Hat

- ☐ Red - 1 skein
- ☐ Orange - 1 skein
- ☐ Green - 1 skein

Crochet Hook

- ☐ Size J (6 mm)
  or size needed for gauge

Additional Supplies

- ☐ Yarn needle (for Hat)

GAUGE INFORMATION

In pattern,

12 sts and 12 rnds = 4" (10 cm)

Gauge Swatch: 4¾" (12 cm) wide (flattened) x 2¼" (5.75 cm) high

With Red, ch 29.

Work same as Cowl for 6 rnds: 15 dc and 7 ch-2 sps.

Finish off.

STITCH GUIDE

SINGLE CROCHET 2 TOGETHER

(abbreviated sc2tog)

Pull up a loop in each of next 2 sts, YO and draw through all 3 loops on hook **(counts as one sc)**.

INSTRUCTIONS

Cowl

With Red, ch 169; being careful not to twist ch, join with slip st to back ridge of first ch to form a ring *(Fig. 1, page 44)*.

Rnd 1 (Right side)**:** Ch 1, sc in back ridge of same st as joining and each ch around; join with slip st to first sc: 169 sc.

Note: Loop a short piece of yarn around any stitch to mark Rnd 1 as **right** side.

The **right** side will always be facing you. When changing colors, drop unused yarn to **back** of work. Carry yarn loosely along inside of piece; do **not** cut yarn until specified.

Rnd 2: Ch 3 **(counts as first dc, now and throughout)**, ★ dc in next 2 sc, ch 2, skip next 2 sc; repeat from ★ around; join with slip st to first dc changing to Orange *(Fig. A)*; do **not** cut Red: 85 dc and 42 ch-2 sps.

Fig. A

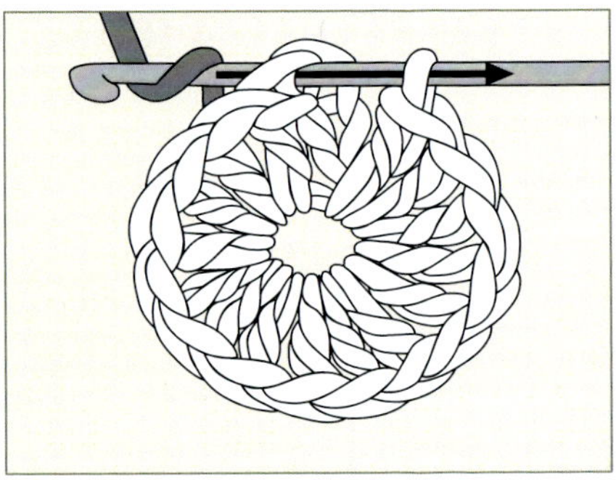

When instructed to work dc in each of 2 skipped sts one rnd **below**, work **around** ch-2 of previous rnd *(Fig. 5, page 45)*.

Rnd 3: Ch 5 **(counts as first dc plus ch 2, now and throughout)**, skip next 2 dc, dc in next 2 skipped dc one rnd **below**, ★ ch 2, skip next 2 dc, dc in next 2 skipped dc one rnd **below**; repeat from ★ around changing to Green in last dc made *(Fig. B)*; join with slip st to first dc.

Fig. B

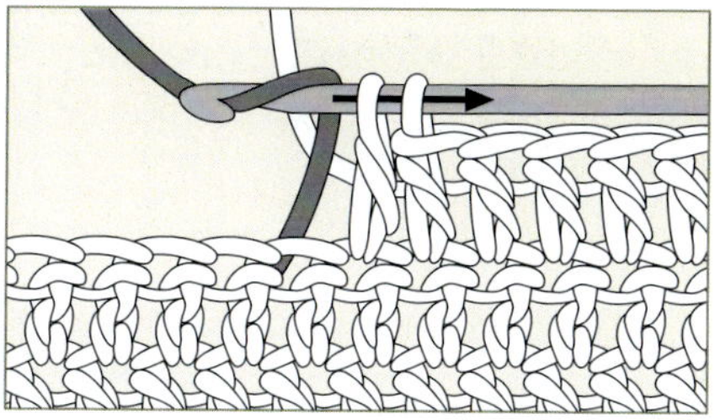

Work in the following color sequence: Green, Red, ★ one rnd **each** of Orange, Green, Red; repeat from ★ for sequence.

Rnd 4: Ch 3, ★ dc in next 2 skipped dc one rnd **below**, ch 2, skip next 2 dc; repeat from ★ around; join with slip st to first dc changing to next color.

Rnd 5: Ch 5, skip next 2 dc, dc in next 2 skipped dc one rnd **below**, ★ ch 2, skip next 2 dc, dc in next 2 skipped dc one rnd **below**; repeat from ★ around changing to next color in last dc made; join with slip st to first dc.

Rnds 6-19: Repeat Rnds 4 and 5, 7 times.

Rnd 20: Ch 1, sc in same st as joining, ★ dc in next 2 skipped dc one row **below**, sc in next 2 dc; repeat from ★ around; join with slip st to first sc, finish off: 169 sts.

Hat

With Red, ch 61 loosely; being careful not to twist ch, join with slip st to back ridge of first ch to form a ring *(Fig. 1, page 44)*.

Rnd 1 (Right side)**:** Ch 1, sc in back ridge of same st as joining and each ch around; join with slip st to first sc: 61 sc.

The **right** side will always be facing you. When changing colors, drop unused yarn to **back** of work. Carry yarn loosely along inside of piece; do **not** cut yarn until specified.

Rnd 2: Ch 3 **(counts as first dc, now and throughout)**, ★ dc in next 2 sc, ch 2, skip next 2 sc; repeat from ★ around; join with slip st to first dc changing to Orange *(Fig. A, page 34)*; do **not** cut Red: 31 dc and 15 ch-2 sps.

When instructed to work dc in each of 2 skipped sts one rnd **below**, work **around** ch-2 of previous rnd *(Fig. 5, page 45)*.

Rnd 3: Ch 5 **(counts as first dc plus ch 2, now and throughout)**, skip next 2 dc, dc in next 2 skipped sc one rnd **below**, ★ ch 2, skip next 2 dc, dc in next 2 skipped sc one rnd **below**; repeat from ★ around changing to Green in last dc made *(Fig. B, page 35)*; join with slip st to first dc.

Work in the following color sequence: Green, Red, ★ one rnd **each** of Orange, Green, Red; repeat from ★ for sequence.

Rnd 4: Ch 3, ★ dc in next 2 skipped dc one rnd **below**, ch 2, skip next 2 dc; repeat from ★ around; join with slip st to first dc changing to next color.

Rnd 5: Ch 5, skip next 2 dc, dc in next 2 skipped dc one rnd **below**, ★ ch 2, skip next 2 dc, dc in next 2 skipped dc one rnd **below**; repeat from ★ around changing to next color in last dc made; join with slip st to first dc.

Rnds 6-19: Repeat Rnds 4 and 5, 7 times.

Rnd 20: Ch 1, sc in same st as joining, ★ dc in next 2 skipped dc one rnd **below**, sc in next 2 dc; repeat from ★ around; join with slip st to first sc, finish off: 61 sts.

CROWN

Rnd 1: Ch 1, skip same st as joining, (sc2tog, sc in next 8 sts) around; join with slip st to first sc: 54 sc.

Rnd 2: Ch 1, beginning in same st as joining, (sc2tog, sc in next 7 sc) around; join with slip st to first sc: 48 sc.

Rnd 3: Ch 1, beginning in same st as joining, (sc2tog, sc in next 6 sc) around; join with slip st to first sc: 42 sc.

Rnd 4: Ch 1, beginning in same st as joining, (sc2tog, sc in next 5 sc) around; join with slip st to first sc: 36 sc.

Rnd 5: Ch 1, beginning in same st as joining, (sc2tog, sc in next 4 sc) around; join with slip st to first sc: 30 sc.

Rnd 6: Ch 1, beginning in same st as joining, (sc2tog, sc in next 3 sc) around; join with slip st to first sc: 24 sc.

Rnd 7: Ch 1, beginning in same st as joining, (sc2tog, sc in next 2 sc) around; join with slip st to first sc: 18 sc.

Rnd 8: Ch 1, beginning in same st as joining, (sc2tog, sc in next sc) around; join with slip st to first sc: 12 sc.

Rnd 9: Ch 1, beginning in same st as joining, sc2tog around; join with slip st to first sc, finish off leaving a long end for sewing: 6 sc.

Thread yarn needle with long end and weave needle through sts on Rnd 9 ***(Fig. 6, page 45)***; pull tightly to close and secure end.

Two-Way Button-Up Cowl

EASY

Finished Size: 7" high x 28" long (18 cm x 71 cm)

SHOPPING LIST

Yarn (Medium Weight) 4

[3.5 ounces, 170 yards
(100 grams, 156 meters) per skein]:

- ☐ 1 skein

Crochet Hook

- ☐ Size I (5.5 mm)
  or size needed for gauge

Additional Supplies

- ☐ $1^3/_8$" (35 mm) Buttons - 3
- ☐ Sewing needle and matching thread

GAUGE INFORMATION

In pattern,
2 repeats = 4½" (11.5 cm)

Gauge Swatch:
7" wide x 4½" high
(17.75 cm x 11.5 cm)

Work same as Cowl for 8 rows:
28 dc and 3 sc.

INSTRUCTIONS

Ch 23.

Row 1: Sc in second ch from hook and in next 2 chs, ★ ch 3, skip next 2 chs, sc in next 5 chs; repeat from ★ once **more**, ch 3, skip next 2 chs, sc in last 3 chs: 16 sc and 3 ch-3 sps.

Row 2 (Right side)**:** Ch 1, turn; sc in first sc, ★ 9 dc in next ch-3 sp, skip next 2 sc, sc in next sc; repeat from ★ 2 times **more**: 27 dc and 4 sc.

Note: Loop a short piece of yarn around any stitch to mark Row 2 as **right** side.

Row 3: Ch 4 **(counts as first dc plus ch 1)**, turn; skip next 2 dc, sc in next 5 dc, ★ ch 3, skip next 5 sts, sc in next 5 dc; repeat from ★ once **more**, ch 1, skip next 2 dc, dc in last sc: 17 sts and 4 sps.

Row 4: Ch 3 **(counts as first dc)**, turn; 4 dc in first dc, skip next 2 sc, sc in next sc, ★ 9 dc in next ch-3 sp, skip next 2 sc, sc in next sc; repeat from ★ once **more**, skip next 2 sc and last ch-1 sp, 5 dc in last dc: 28 dc and 3 sc.

Row 5: Ch 1, turn; sc in first 3 dc, ★ ch 3, skip next 5 sts, sc in next 5 dc; repeat from ★ once **more**, ch 3, skip next 5 sts, sc in last 3 dc: 16 sc and 3 ch-3 sps.

Row 6: Ch 1, turn; sc in first sc, ★ 9 dc in next ch-3 sp, skip next 2 sc, sc in next sc; repeat from ★ 2 times **more**: 27 dc and 4 sc.

Repeat Rows 3-6 for pattern until piece measures approximately 27" (68.5 cm) from beginning ch, ending by working Row 4.

Last Row: Ch 1, turn; sc in first 3 dc, ★ ch 2, skip next 5 sts, sc in next 5 dc; repeat from ★ once **more**, ch 2, skip next 5 sts, sc in last 3 dc: 16 sc and 3 ch-2 sps.

Trim: Ch 1, turn; 3 sc in first sc, sc in next 2 sc, 2 sc in next ch-2 sp, (sc in next 5 sc, 2 sc in next ch-2 sp) twice, sc in next 2 sc, 3 sc in last sc; sc evenly across ends of rows; working in free loops of beginning ch *(Fig. 3, page 44)*, 3 sc in ch at base of first sc, sc in next 2 chs, 2 sc in next ch-2 sp, (sc in next 5 chs, 2 sc in next ch-2 sp) twice, sc in next 2 chs, 3 sc in last ch; sc evenly across ends of rows; join with slip st to first sc, finish off.

With **right** side facing and using photo as a guide for placement, sew one button at base of each 9-dc group on Row 2.

To wear your Cowl as shown above, use ch-2 sps on last row as buttonholes.

To wear your Cowl as shown on page 39, use spaces formed at the side edge as buttonholes.

General Instructions

ABBREVIATIONS

BPdc	Back Post double crochet(s)
ch(s)	chain(s)
cm	centimeters
dc	double crochet(s)
FP	Front Post
FPdc	Front Post double crochet(s)
hdc	half double crochet(s)
hdc2tog	half double crochet(s) 2 together
mm	millimeters
Rnd(s)	Round(s)
sc	single crochet(s)
sc2tog	single crochet 2 together
sp(s)	space(s)
st(s)	stitch(es)
YO	yarn over

SYMBOLS & TERMS

★ — work instructions following ★ as many **more** times as indicated in addition to the first time.

† to † — work all instructions from first † to second † **as many** times as specified.

( ) or **[ ]** — work enclosed instructions as many times as specified by the number immediately following **or** work all enclosed instructions in the stitch or space indicated **or** contains explanatory remarks.

colon (:) — the number(s) given after a colon at the end of a row or round denote(s) the number of stitches or spaces you should have on that row or round.

CROCHET TERMINOLOGY		
UNITED STATES		INTERNATIONAL
slip stitch (slip st)	=	single crochet (sc)
single crochet (sc)	=	double crochet (dc)
half double crochet (hdc)	=	half treble crochet (htr)
double crochet (dc)	=	treble crochet (tr)
treble crochet (tr)	=	double treble crochet (dtr)
double treble crochet (dtr)	=	triple treble crochet (ttr)
triple treble crochet (tr tr)	=	quadruple treble crochet (qtr)
skip	=	miss

GAUGE

Exact gauge is **essential** for proper size. Before beginning your project, make the sample swatch given in the individual instructions in the yarn and hook specified. After completing the swatch, measure it, counting your stitches and rows/rounds carefully. If your swatch is larger or smaller than specified, **make another, changing hook size to get the correct gauge**. Keep trying until you find the size hook that will give you the specified gauge.

BEGINNER	Projects for first-time crocheters using basic stitches. Minimal shaping.
EASY	Projects using yarn with basic stitches, repetitive stitch patterns, simple color changes, and simple shaping and finishing.
INTERMEDIATE	Projects using a variety of techniques, such as basic lace patterns or color patterns, mid-level shaping and finishing.
EXPERIENCED	Projects with intricate stitch patterns, techniques and dimension, such as non-repeating patterns, multi-color techniques, fine threads, small hooks, detailed shaping and refined finishing.

Yarn Weight Symbol & Names	LACE 0	SUPER FINE 1	FINE 2	LIGHT 3	MEDIUM 4	BULKY 5	SUPER BULKY 6	JUMBO 7
Type of Yarns in Category	Fingering, size 10 crochet thread	Sock, Fingering, Baby	Sport, Baby	DK, Light Worsted	Worsted, Afghan, Aran	Chunky, Craft, Rug	Super Bulky, Roving	Jumbo, Roving
Crochet Gauge* Ranges in Single Crochet to 4" (10 cm)	32-42 sts**	21-32 sts	16-20 sts	12-17 sts	11-14 sts	8-11 sts	6-9 sts	5 sts and fewer
Advised Hook Size Range	Steel*** 6 to 8, Regular hook B-1	B-1 to E-4	E-4 to 7	7 to I-9	I-9 to K-10½	K-10½ to M/N-13	M/N-13 to Q	Q and larger

*GUIDELINES ONLY: The chart above reflects the most commonly used gauges and hook sizes for specific yarn categories.

** Lace weight yarns are usually crocheted with larger hooks to create lacy openwork patterns. Accordingly, a gauge range is difficult to determine. Always follow the gauge stated in your pattern.

*** Steel crochet hooks are sized differently from regular hooks–the higher the number, the smaller the hook, which is the reverse of regular hook sizing.

CROCHET HOOKS	
U.S.	Metric mm
B-1	2.25
C-2	2.75
D-3	3.25
E-4	3.5
F-5	3.75
G-6	4
7	4.5
H-8	5
I-9	5.5
J-10	6
K-10½	6.5
L-11	8
M/N-13	9
N/P-15	10
P/Q	15
Q	16
S	19

JOINING WITH SC

When instructed to join with sc, begin with a slip knot on hook. Insert hook in stitch or space indicated, YO and pull up a loop, YO and draw through both loops on hook.

BACK RIDGE

Work only in loop(s) indicated by arrow *(Fig. 1)*.

Fig. 1

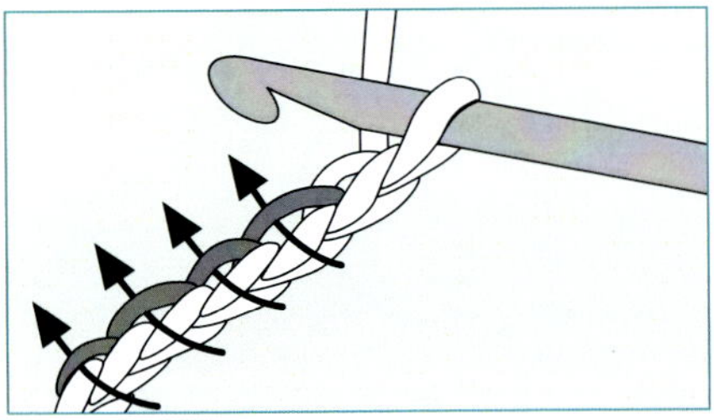

BACK LOOP ONLY

Work only in loop(s) indicated by arrow *(Fig. 2)*.

Fig. 2

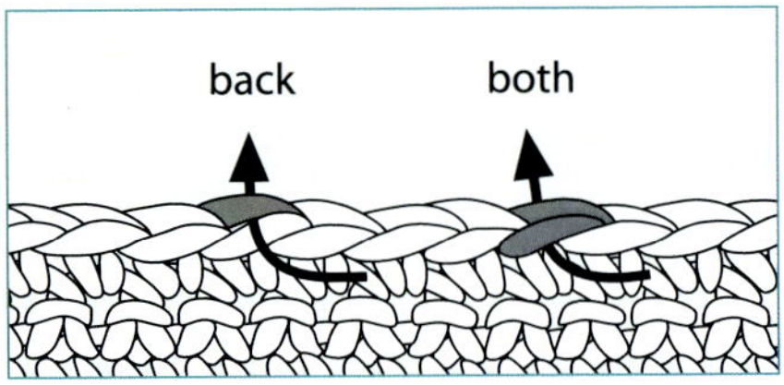

FREE LOOPS OF A CHAIN

When instructed to work in free loops of a chain, work in loop indicated by arrow *(Fig. 3)*.

Fig. 3

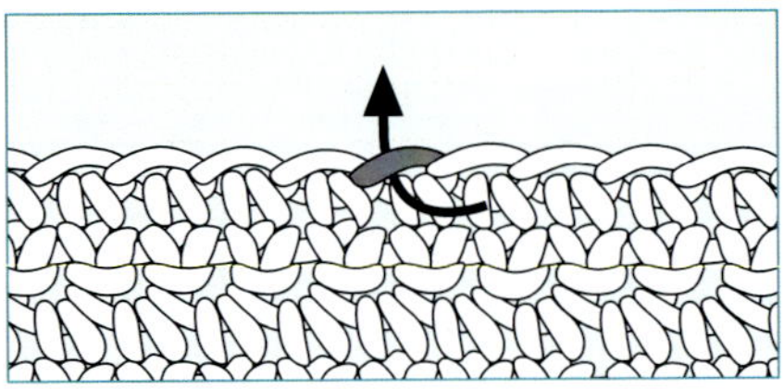

POST STITCH

Work around post of stitch indicated, inserting hook in direction of arrow *(Fig. 4)*.

Fig. 4

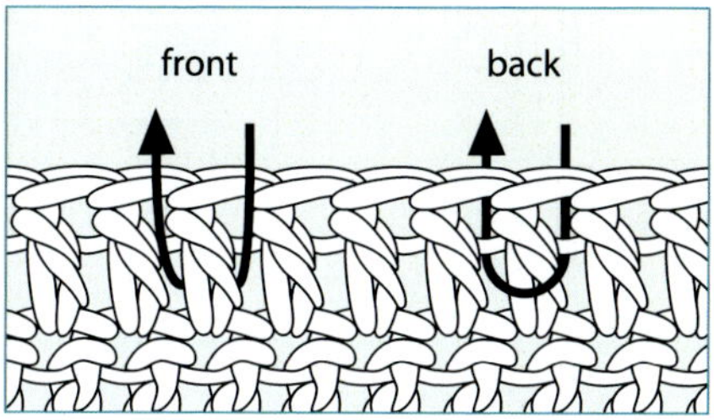

WORKING AROUND CHAINS

Work as indicated by arrow *(Fig. 5)*.

Fig. 5

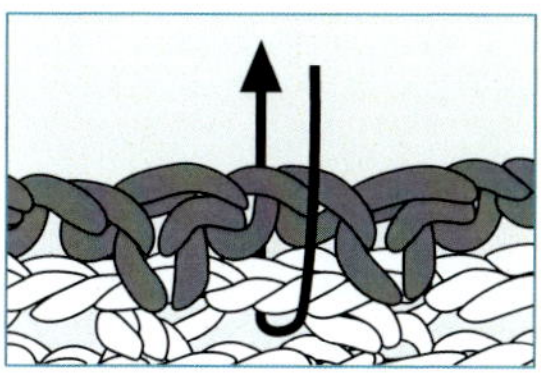

WEAVING THROUGH STITCHES

To close a hole at the top of a hat, thread a yarn needle with the long end left on the last round worked and weave it through the remaining stitches *(Fig. 6)*.

Fig. 6

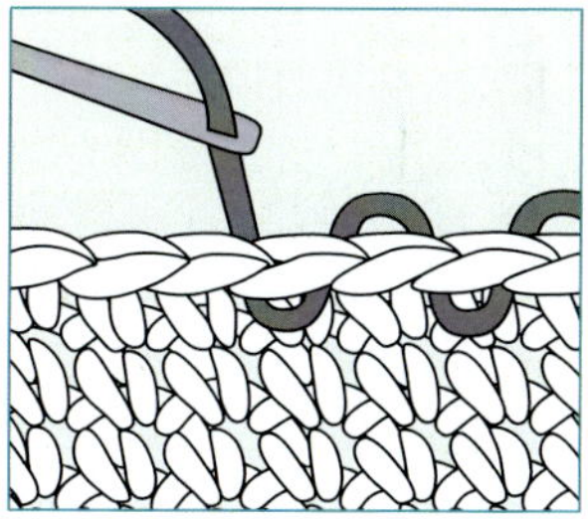

REVERSE SINGLE CROCHET

(abbreviated reverse sc)

Working from **left** to **right**, ★ insert hook in st to right of hook *(Fig. 7a)*, YO and draw through, under and to left of loop on hook (2 loops on hook) *(Fig. 7b)*, YO and draw through both loops on hook *(Fig. 7c)* **(reverse sc made, *Fig. 7d*)**; repeat from ★ around.

Fig. 7a

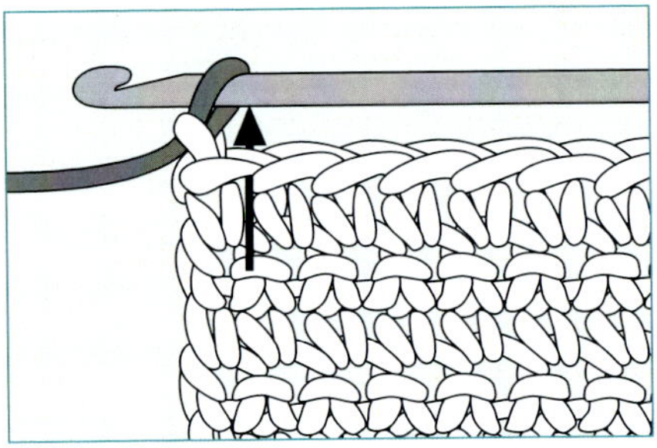

Fig. 7b

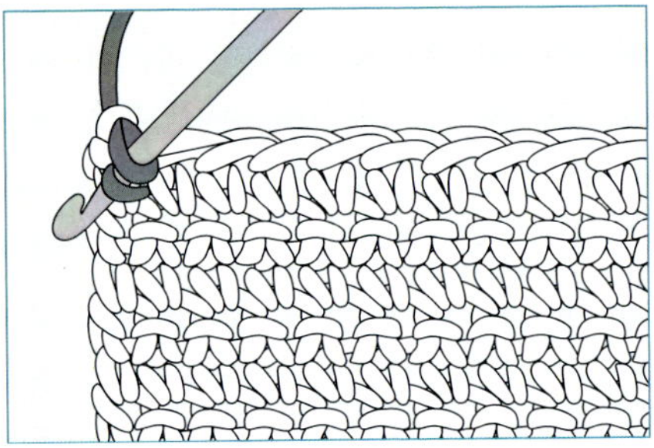

Fig. 7c

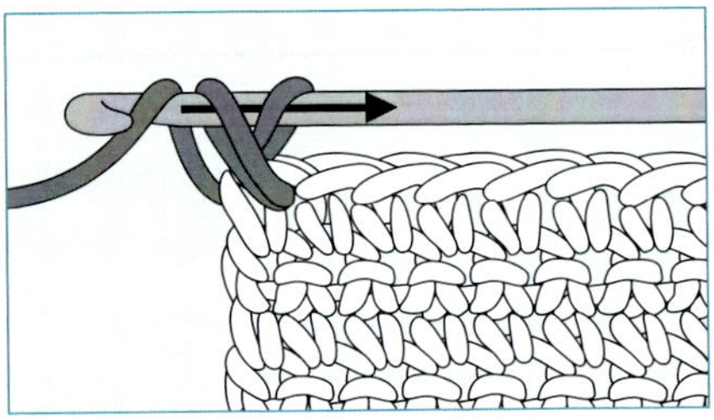

Fig. 7d

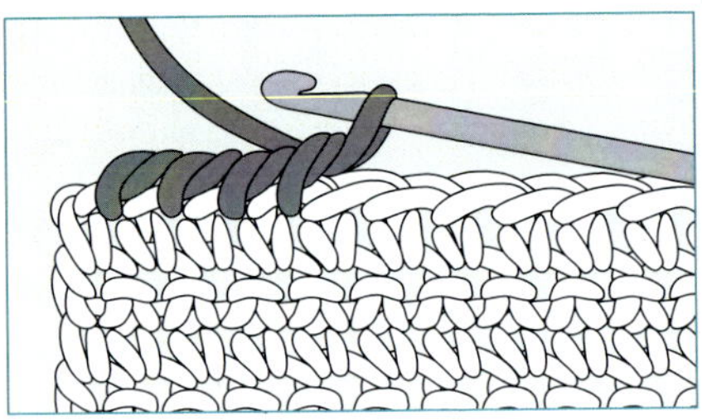

Yarn Information

The projects in this book were made using a variety of yarn weights. Any brand of the specific weight of yarn may be used. It is best to refer to the yardage/meters when determining how many balls or skeins to purchase. Remember, to arrive at the finished size, it is the GAUGE/TENSION that is important, not the brand of yarn.

For your convenience, listed below are the specific yarns used to create our photography models. Because yarn manufacturers make frequent changes in their product lines, you may sometimes find it necessary to use a substitute yarn or to search for the discontinued product at alternate suppliers (locally or online).

BASKET WEAVE SET

Caron® Simply Soft®

#0014 Pagoda

EMBOSSED RIBS SET

Lion Brand® Heartland®

#173 Everglades

FAIR ISLE SET

Patons® Classic Wool Worsted™

Color A - #00225 Dark Grey Mix

Color B - #00226 Black

Color C - #00202 Aran

Color D - #77531 Currant

Color E - #77710 Cherry

Color F - #00208 Burgundy

LITTLE GLITZY NECKWARMER

Red Heart® Boutique Swanky™

#9401 Sterling

SHAPED HAT

Lion Brand® Tweed Stripes®

#208 Wildfire

TWEED SET

Lion Brand® Vanna's Choice®

Red - #133 Brick

Orange - #135 Rust

Green - #174 Olive

TWO-WAY BUTTON-UP COWL

Lion Brand® Vanna's Choice®

#141 Wild Berry

Meet the Designer: Melissa Leapman

With more than 800 knit and crochet designs in print, Melissa Leapman is one of the most widely published American designers working today. Through the years, Leisure Arts has published more than 40 books of Melissa's fabulous designs. Melissa is also the host of several Leisure Arts DVDs in the best-selling teach-yourself series, "I Can't Believe I'm Knitting" and "I Can't Believe I'm Crocheting."

Nationally, her designs have been featured in numerous magazines, and her workshops on knitting and crochet are consistently popular with crafters of all skill levels. She has taught at major events such as STITCHES, Vogue Knitting LIVE, and The Knitting Guild Association conferences, as well as at hundreds of yarn shops and local guild events across the country.

To find more of Melissa's exciting designs, visit LeisureArts.com, "like" Melissa's Facebook page, and join her group (Melissa Leapman Rocks) on Ravelry.com.

We have made every effort to ensure that these instructions are accurate and complete. We cannot, however, be responsible for human error, typographical mistakes, or variations in individual work.

Production Team: Technical Writer/Editor - Lois J. Long; Editorial Writer - Susan Frantz Wiles; Senior Graphic Artist - Lora Puls; Graphic Artist - Frances Huddleston; Photo Stylist - Lori Wenger; and Photographer - Jason Masters.

Items made and instructions tested by Marianna Crowder and Raymelle Greening.

Made in U.S.A.